£6.
C10d/7

CW00734314

HAMPSTEAD HEATH

Deborah Wolton & David McDowall

Photographs by Sandra Lousada

FRANCES LINCOLN LIMITED
PUBLISHERS

For Anne Fraser, whose idea
it was in the first place

British Library Cataloguing in Publication Data
A catalogue record for this book is available from the British Library

ISBN 978-0-7112-2653-1

Designed by Gillian Greenwood

Printed in Singapore

9 8 7 6 5 4 3 2 1

In addition to the 150 open spaces within the square mile, the City of
London owns and manages over 10,000 acres of parks and open spaces in
and around London as part of its commitment to sustaining a world class
city. Each open space is a unique resource managed for the use and
enjoyment of the public and for the conservation of wildlife and historic
landscape. The City of London's commitment to open spaces dates back
to the 1870s, when, in response to the rapid disappearance of many public
open areas to make way for the building of new suburban homes and city
offices, it embarked on an ambitious project to safeguard some of what
remained. Parks and open spaces managed by the City of London include
Hampstead Heath, Epping Forest, Burnham Beeches, Ashstead Common,
West Ham Park, Queen's Park and Highgate Wood.

CONTENTS

N

W   E

S

HEATH
EXTENSION

GOLDERS GREEN
STATION

HAMPSTEAD LANE

KENWOOD

HAMPSTEAD WAY

WILDWOOD ROAD

NORTH END

GOLDERS HILL PARK

SANDY
HEATH

WEST HEATH

SPANIARDS ROAD

EAST PARK

97m

VALE
OF
HEALTH

EAST HEATH

WEST HEATH ROAD

HEATH STREET

HAMPSTEAD

WELL WALK

WILLOW ROAD

NEW END

KEATS GROVE

DOWNSHIRE HILL

HAMPSTEAD
STATION

GRAVEL OR PAVED PATHS

FOOT PATHS

BUILDINGS

SPORTS AND PLAY AREAS

0   100   200   300   400   500

METRES

HAMPSTEAD HEATH

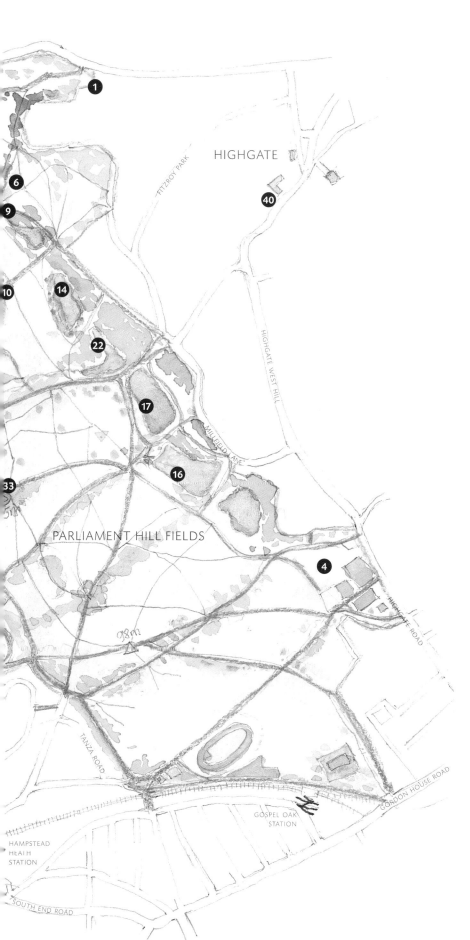

1. Athlone House
2. Boundary Path
3. Cohen's Fields
4. Dukes Field
5. Fairground sites
6. Goodison Fountain
7. Hampstead Gate
8. Hampstead Ponds
9. Highgate Brook
10. Highgate Gate
11. Inverforth House
12. Iron Pan Ponds
13. Kenwood House
14. Ladies' Bathing Pond
15. Leg o'Mutton Pond
16. Men's Bathing Pond
17. Model Boating Pond
18. North Wood
19. Old Wyldes
20. Pasture Ground
21. Pergola

22. Sanctuary Pond
23. Seven Sisters Ponds
24. South Meadow
25. South Wood
26. Spaniards Inn
27. Sports ground
28. The Dairy
29. The Hill Garden
30. The Paddock
31. The Pound
32. Thousand Pound Pond
33. Tumulus
34. Turner's Wood
35. Unwin's Great Wall
36. Vale of Health Pond
37. Viaduct Pond
38. West Meadow
39. Whitestone Pond
40. Witanhurst
41. Wood Pond

INTRODUCTION

There can be few Londoners who have never set foot on Hampstead Heath, for it is the Londoner's open space par excellence, their substitute countryside. Or is it? The Heath seems to exist in its own definition, with neither the countryside nor London's parks quite matching it. Many of us who live within a stone's throw of the Heath know it like the back of our hand. We routinely walk there. Or perhaps we explored it as children. And we are sure we know it, every inch. Or do we? Most of us have a tendency to walk the same routes, and look at the same things. In thinking we know the Heath intimately, it is easy to miss some of the less obvious delights that lie in wait. When we first looked at the Heath with a view to writing about it, we, the authors, found ourselves suddenly more ignorant that we had ever imagined. We hope that as you read this book and enjoy the photography, you too will experience flashes of recognition of things perhaps half-noticed but not before quite appre-hended, and possibly like us discover things entirely new to you. Moreover, we hope to introduce you to some of the colourful characters who played a part in the story of the Heath.

Few think of the Heath as wild, but then there is virtually no English countryside that is wild in a true sense either. Even on the uplands of the Yorkshire Dales or the Lake District, man's controlling hand is very evident in a landscape carefully maintained by grazing. If it were not so, these landscapes would be quickly covered in scrub and trees. Indeed, those who have rambled the Heath for over fifty years will know how much more overgrown and 'feral' it is now, despite being more heavily trampled by Londoners, than it was in, say, 1950.

One of the Seven Sisters Ponds, the wildest corner of the Heath Extension and an excellent habitat for dragonflies and damselflies

ABOVE A William Morris-like
pattern of frosty buttercups on
the damper lower slopes
LEFT Since the late 1980s the
regime of relentless mowing has
been reduced, bringing great
benefit to wildlife and a delightful
variety of colour and texture.

Furthermore, the land has been put to a variety of uses, some of them now quite surprising. For example, in the early years of the twentieth century, South Meadow was a golf course, played upon by no less a personage that Czar Nicholas II's younger brother, the Grand Duke Michael Alexandrovich. And who now remembers the ski-jump?

How the Heath has been used and managed has always aroused the ire of those who have strongly held but trenchantly different views. For some there is immense irritation at the way the sycamore saplings are allowed to flourish 'like weeds'. Others have been upset by the mowing of the long grass, an issue that came to a head in the late 1970s. When a *Times* journalist questioned the necessity of relentless mowing, he received the startling riposte from a harassed official:

> That's all very well, but what about the dead bodies? . . . Do you realise there are 20 corpses hidden around the Heath every year? . . . We can't just expect them to rot away.

Hilarity apart, to appreciate Hampstead Heath the landscape can usefully be divided into topographical compartments, not those created by its barriers of tarmac and cars but those that reflect the three principal ways the landscape has traditionally been used. Along the top of the Heath are the last vestiges of true heathland, which once spread across West Heath and Sandy Heath and straddled the Spaniards Road. Much of it has lost its characteristic identity because of the growth of trees and scrub over the past century. Then there is long-established woodland, of which the North and South Woods of Kenwood are virtually the only survivors of a much more extensive tree-covered landscape. Finally, there are the ghosts of farmland, which has been predominantly pasture and meadow during the past 500 years. Despite the encroachment of secondary woodland, it is astonishing how these three types of land use are still highly visible today.

If you are wondering how land use was decided upon, well over a thousand years ago, the answer lies, of course, beneath the soil and the flora, with the geology of the place.

GEOLOGY

Your self-esteem will immediately be dented on learning that the very first person publicly to acknowledge that geology underpinned any understanding of the Heath was a nineteen year-old stripling. In his magisterial work *Topography and Natural History of Hampstead*, published in 1814, John Park observed that

> It has frequently been asked 'Why is the sand of Hampstead confined to its heath? How is it that we do not find sand in digging in our fields? Or what is there in the nature of a heath, which should make it the exclusive depository of such a substance?'

These were questions which must have been asked any number of times over preceding centuries, or even millennia. Park, however, was the first on record to offer accurate answers:

> It is not, I would say, that the sand is confined to the heath but, *e converso*, that the heath is confined to the sand, or more fully thus: a certain portion of the land has, by some operation of nature, which we suppose to be the action of a pre-existent ocean, been covered with a bed of sand.

Park's first observation would not have surprised the people who first started to clear the woodland that grew on the sand over seven thousand years earlier. But his second comment, about a pre-existent ocean, would have stopped many people of his own day in their tracks. Perhaps Park had read the ground-breaking work of the geologist James Hutton, who had theorized in the 1780s that sedimentary rock must have been consolidated on the seabed and then uplifted to form land. If so, it might have helped Park hit upon the fundamental truth about the Heath, that it is composed of a simple succession of layers, without faults or folds, all laid down by water.

Once one has appreciated, in Park's footsteps, that each layer has its own characteristics, other things make sense. The top layer is a deposit of sand, with some overlying deposits of pebble gravel, and rises to some 420 feet above London. It lies in an arc from the upper slopes of Fitzjohn's Avenue in Hampstead along the axis of the Spaniards Road and Hampstead Lane to Highgate.

ABOVE Sand and pebbles deposited 40 million years ago by a vast river flowing from the west
OPPOSITE Upturned roots reveal the Bagshot Sand.

This capping is a sandbank laid down approximately 40
million years ago, the deposit of a vast river flowing from the
west. We know this because the sand contains particles of
granite from Devon. It is known as Bagshot Sand, after the
location in west Surrey where this deposit was first identified. It
is pure, fine-grained sand, high in iron salts, and ranges in colour
from buff to deep orange. It contains several seams of pebbles,
the residue of flood episodes while the sand was being laid
down. Such pebbles are found not merely on the high ground
where they were originally laid but all over the Heath, since they
have been washed downhill by rainfall or by erosion. The sand
and gravel create acid soils of low fertility from an agricultural
point of view but of the greatest interest for the botanist,
entomologist and ecologist.

The sand itself proved of great value for building, for filling in
the many potholes in London's streets and more recently for
filling sandbags in two world wars. The dips and hollows over
many parts of the upper Heath are the result of sand and gravel
digging over centuries; the first mention of this is in Gerard's
Herball, 1597, in which he describes a 'gravell pit' near the
Whitestone Pond. The commoners' right to dig for sand and
gravel was disputed by the Lord of the Manor in 1780 but the
case before the Court of the King's Bench was decided in favour
of the copyholders (or commoners), 'who will continue as usual
to open pits and cut turf.'

The removal of sand from Sandy Heath moved onto an
altogether different scale in the 1860s when the Lord of the
Manor, Sir Thomas Maryon Wilson, frustrated in his plans to
develop parts of the Heath, resorted to other ways of
'converting it to my own profit'. He proceeded to sell hundreds

LEFT Bog plants growing
on the spring line between
sand and clay
RIGHT Two oak survivors
of the 1860s sand
extraction

of thousands of tons of sand to the Midland Railway Company for the extension of its line to St Pancras. To give you some idea of the huge quantity of sand that was removed, before the excavations Sandy Heath was level with the Spaniards Road. In 1871 the *Illustrated London News* reported:

> The very body of the earth has been cut away to an amazing depth . . . Holes are scooped out close to the high road thirty or forty feet deep, and big enough to bury the corpses of a nation for half a century . . . but ugly enough to deter the boldest survivor from approaching so ghastly a spot.

Trees have now colonized most of Sandy Heath but there is still something strange and eerie about it.

Below the sand is the very variable layer of sand and loam known as Claygate Beds, named after another Surrey location, which is usually sandy and acid at the top and progressively more clayish and neutral below. As water drains freely through the upper layers of sand and meets a layer of clay it moves horizontally, seeping or 'springing' out of sloping ground. This is why one is forever treading in unexpected muddy patches on the hilly parts of the Heath. You can sometimes feel underfoot the change in the geology from 'springy' sand to more solid heavier ground, and

ABOVE AND OPPOSITE The acidic bog on West Meadow is carefully managed to conserve the interesting bog flora.

there is usually a clear change in the flora, the fine-bladed grasses and acid-loving plants of the sand giving way to coarser bladed and darker green grasses of the more clayish and moister soils. The variability of the Claygate Beds is well demonstrated in a gully in West Meadow, where an acidic bog has developed on a patch of impervious clay. This is the only place in London where you can find sphagnum moss, more usually found on the moors of Scotland. Elsewhere on the Heath these 'flushes' or damp patches provide the conditions for interesting communities of plants such as the yellow iris and water mint that can be found in the middle of the meadow west of the Ladies' Pond.

The lower parts of the Heath sit on London Clay, a layer 345 feet thick of the fine silty mud deposited 60 million yeas ago in warm sea. Below the London Clay are about 575 feet of chalk and below that lies Devonian rock. The former agricultural landscapes of the Heath, the pasture fields and hay meadows of Parliament Hill and the Heath Extension with their enclosing hedgerows coincide with the richer, neutral soils of the lower parts of the Claygate Beds and London Clay – land that never was 'heath'. It was these rustic pastures and meadows that the London County Council (LCC), in the early years of the twentieth century, tried to 'parkify', by pulling out some hedgerows and

Humphry Repton proposed clearing away the enclosed gardens of Kenwood in the 1790s to create an elegant sweeping lawn. Water seeps out at the junction of the Bagshot Sand and Claygate Beds to form this little stream.

planting clumps of ornamental trees, red and other exotic oaks, and copper beeches. Their policy was one of 'tidying up' the Heath. There were howls of protest. 'Parkification' has always been the greatest fear for Heath lovers. Octavia Hill summed that fear up in an article in the *Daily Graphic* in 1890:

> The late Metropolitan Board [in charge of the Heath before the LCC took over in 1889] . . . left Hampstead Heath unfenced, and in the main, wild and undisturbed . . . Cannot they [the LCC] understand that what people who go as far as Hampstead seek is, not the formality of the London Park . . . but something of a freer space where the wild flowers and meadow slopes may be seen in their natural condition.

TOP LEFT, AND RIGHT The emergence of a spring in Ladies' Pond Meadow provides the conditions for a community of damp-loving plants: nettle, foxglove, Yorkshire fog and iris.

BOTTOM LEFT Sphagnum moss, a rarity in south-east England, is found in West Meadow and West Heath. It requires acidic, permanently wet and nutrient-poor soil.

WATER

John Park talked of 'a pre-existing ocean', but water has always had a crucial relationship with the geology of the Heath. Water flow shaped the Heath. A vast river deposited the capping of sand, and torrents of water from the glacial ice sheet in the last ice age cut the gullies and formed the valleys. Moreover, it was the special qualities of Hampstead's water that initially brought people out of London to live here, the self-confident professional classes who eventually saved the Heath from development.

Rainwater drains west, north and south from the high ground. The western side of Hampstead, some way from the Heath, drains into the River Kilburn, known further downstream as the Westbourne before it enters the Thames near Chelsea Bridge. To the north the Heath's water drains into two main streams, one via the Leg o' Mutton Pond on West Heath, through Golders Hill, and the other further east, through the Seven Sisters Ponds on the Heath Extension. Both run into the River Brent and thence down the Brent valley into the Thames at Brentford.

On the south side of the Hampstead–Highgate ridge, two brooks, both springing from under the Bagshot Sand, run down the respective Hampstead and Highgate sides of the Heath. Before they were piped underground, these two streams met in Kentish Town to form the River Fleet or more anciently the Holebourne (Holborn as we know it today) or 'stream in the hollow'. The headwaters of the Fleet now seem modest trickles. Yet in the early nineteenth century the Highgate Brook was still 13 feet wide where it crossed the Highgate road just beside Dukes Field. An anchor has been found in the riverbed in lower

Viaduct Pond

Kentish Town, suggesting it might once have been navigable up to the confluence of the streams. Yet a journey up the Fleet was anything but a fragrant experience. In the late sixteenth century Ben Jonson described just such a voyage, observing the seat of every privy 'fill'd with buttock and the walls do sweat urine and plaisters', while every oar stroke 'belched forth an ayre as hot as the muster of all your night tubs'. Be distracted from this distressing thought by the knowledge that up to the late nineteenth century the crystal springs of Parliament Hill, East Heath and New End fed watercress beds where now the North London Line runs and also at the bottom of Downshire Hill.

When potable supplies became insufficient for the growing population, it was to these springs that the authorities turned. In 1544 Henry VIII's parliament provided for the tapping of the headwaters of the Fleet, and the City Corporation, which had been charged with responsibility for adequate potable supplies since the thirteenth century, was duly empowered to lay pipes, dig pits and erect conduits to exploit the springs on the Heath. Almost 150 years later, in 1692, the City Corporation leased the Hampstead springs to the Hampstead Water Company. New ponds were dug: first the Hampstead Ponds and then the Highgate Ponds. Pipes made of hollowed elm were used to convey the water, remains of which were found below the Highgate Ponds during excavations in the mid-nineteenth century. Another was found above the Viaduct Pond in the 1970s. The earliest pond to be dug was, in all probability, a reservoir below the present Hampstead Ponds alongside South End Road, where there is now a grove of lofty planes and limes. This pond was abandoned after it became putrid. It was filled with spoil in 1892 and trees were planted.

Nesting swans in the Vale of Health

The Vale of Health Pond was a late addition, dug in 1777. The Vale of Health, known before the early nineteenth century less glamorously as Hatchett's Bottom, was once an unhealthy swamp on the common where one Samuel Hatch, harness and collarmaker, was granted a plot of land, no doubt as an encouragement to move his malodorous business away from the highway and other dwellings. While everyone else spurned living in so unpleasant and putrid a place, Hatch must have lived a very solitary life. Once drained, however, the little hamlet rapidly became a desirable place to live and was renamed the Vale of Health in defiance of its previous reputation.

Almost all ponds are manmade and usually fed by a stream or spring. Unless dug into impervious clay, they have to be lined or 'puddled'. Puddling is the labour-intensive but effective precursor to butyl rubber. Clay is laid to form the base of the pond and 'trodden in', an arduous task rather like kneading bread, to form a compressed and impervious membrane. Sheep or other livestock were often driven on to such clay layers to

Model Boating Pond

assist the process. Lower down the hillside, puddling would have been less arduous, because the clay was already in place. But ponds higher up the hill, for example Wood Pond and Thousand Pound Pond just below Kenwood House, probably required the carting of substantial quantities of clay in order to lay and then puddle an impervious lining.

The Hampstead and Highgate Ponds continued to supply water to Kentish Town and Camden Town for 150 years until they could no longer keep pace with the rapidly increasing demand. By the 1830s the yield from the ponds was insufficient and a well was sunk to a depth of 400 feet at the foot of East Heath Road beside the lowest, Hampstead no. 1 Pond (opposite the end of Keats Grove). A steam pump brought water to the surface, housed in an octagonal tower which was demolished in 1907, fifteen years after the demise of the pond.

Very much more mysterious ponds lie on top of Sandy Heath. They are partly the accidental result of sand extraction. Being more or less at the summit of the Heath they are neither stream nor spring fed, nor do they drain away, in spite of the fact that sand could hardly be more porous. The secret of these strange ponds lies in one of the qualities of the Bagshot Sand. It has heavy iron content and in this particular case iron oxide has assisted the coalescence of the sand into a hard crust of sandstone, known as an iron pan, lying about 3 feet beneath the surface. It is difficult to explain the apparently healthy oaks growing out of one of the ponds, except as predating the sand extraction.

The Seven Sisters Ponds were dug by unemployed labourers, 1908–9.
Marsh marigolds (left) and common reeds (right)

On the north side of the Hampstead–Highgate watershed one of the two streams feeds the Seven Sisters Ponds of the Heath Extension. The highest of these ponds is at least 150 years old. The rest were dug in 1908–9 by unemployed labourers. On the course of the other north-flowing stream through West Heath, the Leg o' Mutton Pond was dug during an earlier and similar poor relief programme. In the years following the Napoleonic Wars there was widespread depression and severe unemployment. Hampstead set up its own relief programme in about 1816 and unemployed labourers were set to work on the Heath, 'improving' the landscape. Some, who thought they could benefit financially, were delighted. An advertisement in *The Times* announced:

> By a subscription from the inhabitants of Hampstead, according to their accustomed liberality, for employing on the roads poor men out of work, the Heath is now become not only a pleasant and delightful promenade for the inhabitants, but highly beneficial and amusing to the pupils of Mr. BALLANTINE'S Classical and Commercial Academy.

Others were less delighted, as is almost always the case on the Heath. Another contemporary newspaper article expostulated:

> Will it be believed that at this moment there are near fourscore of these parish pioneers busily engaged with spades, shovels, pickaxes, wheelbarrows and all the implements of rural destruction, in shaving, levelling, embanking and turfing Hampstead Heath?

> All those rude hillocks – sudden breaks – abrupt banks, and bold inequalities with their varied tints of soil, and verdure, and of plants, which form the pre-ground of this extensive and picturesque view, the admiration of foreigners, and the delightful study of our artists, are in danger of being reduced to a tame, formal, vapid smoothness, by the rash hands of tasteless improvers.

> Nor is this all – for it is said that these well meaning projectors, these new arbiters of taste, have it in contemplation to make – yes to make – an artificial piece of water on the north-west side of the Heath.

LEFT AND RIGHT Coots always seem to succeed in getting the good nesting sites.
ABOVE Highgate Brook, a tributary of the Fleet
BOTTOM RIGHT Water forget-me-nots

In spite of this outburst of outrage the work went ahead and it is probable that the 'artificial piece of water' was the Leg o' Mutton Pond on West Heath. Of course, the heath then was not the large area we call the Heath today. Nor was it a public open space. It was the Common of the Manor of Hampstead and obviously even at this early date it was cherished for its roughness and wildness. The episode was an indication of the way the Heath was already valued more for its recreational value than as heathland grazing.

Water, of course, sustains wildlife and this comes in myriad forms. For example, a remarkable number of dragonflies and damselflies live off the Seven Sisters Ponds; occasionally one catches the turquoise flash of a kingfisher on the Sanctuary Pond. Elsewhere in many parts, the damp patches, where water seeps from under the sand, support communities of wetland plants quite distinct from the rest of the Heath's flora.

Nor should we discount human life, drawn to take the unusual waters here. The water of the Bagshot Sand varies enormously. In some places Hampstead's springs produce pure, soft and lime-free water. Elsewhere the water has an iron salt content in the form of iron carbonate, iron oxide and iron sulphate. Known as 'chalybeate', these waters were, according to John Park, 'of the same nature and equal in virtue with Tunbridge Wells' and taken as a purgative. The distinctive rust-brown colour of chalybeate water is still evident in several places on the Heath, for example in the water feeding Wood Pond, below Kenwood House, and also in that running through the Goodison Fountain, discolouring its stonework.

Hampstead's healthy water transformed what was a small village on the way to St Albans into a thriving spa. In 1698 Hampstead's Lady of the Manor granted to trustees acting for the parish poor six acres of the Heath containing springs to erect spa buildings. It was not long before an even larger area from New End down more or less to Willow Road had been built upon. Soon, Londoners were flocking to Hampstead Wells to take the waters. The fashion for taking Hampstead's spa water persisted for much of the eighteenth century. In 1734 a medical practitioner, Dr Soame, proudly announced he 'had experienced relief in a most obstinate and painful case of stone by use of its waters, and that he constantly shaved in them'. What better recommendation could one ask for?

LEFT Wood Pond, Kenwood
TOP RIGHT A crow on Sandy Heath
BOTTOM RIGHT The rust-red of a chalybeate stream

HEATHLAND

Heathland occurs on well-drained, acid soil and it occurs here upon the great bank of Bagshot Sand between Hampstead and Highgate. Except in a few cases, heathland is artificial, not natural. Here, on Hampstead Heath, it was created by clearing the land of its tree and shrub cover and grazing livestock. Most heaths are ancient, often going back to Neolithic or even Mesolithic times, up to nine thousand years ago. That a Mesolithic site has been found on West Heath strongly suggests that the origins of the Heath are that old.

Over the years grazing livestock leave a changed flora of bracken, heather, broom, gorse and acid-loving fine-bladed grasses. When grazing stops, however, trees and scrub encroach again and this is what to a very great extent has occurred on Hampstead Heath, as on most heaths across northern Europe. The decline began about three centuries ago, when agricultural improvement and specialization reduced the use of heathland. Nevertheless, this heath remained heath right up to the late nineteenth century, and continued to be the haunt of footpads, who found plenty of cover from which to mount an ambush on vulnerable travellers.

Much of Hampstead's heathland began to be lost with the loss of grazing animals in the nineteenth century, when it came into public ownership. The signs are all over West and Sandy Heaths: large mature birch trees, which are renowned for colonizing open acid ground. One could probably date the decline of Hampstead's heath precisely from the tree rings of the older birches. One need only look at Constable's many

West Heath. When grazing stops, birch is one of the first trees to colonize heathland.

LEFT Undulating ground, the result of sand-digging on Sandy Heath

ABOVE AND OPPOSITE Heather and bracken, characteristic plants of heathland

paintings of Hampstead Heath, executed mainly in the 1820s, to see what a different landscape it once was. Birches were among the first to take advantage of the absence of livestock, which would otherwise have cropped virtually every tree seedling. Some older oak and beech trees, slower growing than the birch, indicate they too escaped the attentions of grazers, by either growing inside a thicket, or having been protected by human intervention.

In the Middle Ages heathland was often described as 'the common waste'. This was land on which the manorial tenants were allowed to graze the one or two animals they might own. They could also harvest gorse, heather, bracken and grass turfs which provided fuel, kindling, bedding and building materials. They were rationed in these assets by the Manor steward. This was to ensure enough for the Lord of the Manor and to conserve the overall asset for future years. A tenant's ration was known as a 'stint'. During the thirteenth century some of the heathland was almost certainly turned into agricultural land, in response to the rise in population and therefore food demand. Reclamation of the waste took place all over England at this time. But the dreadful weather of the fourteenth century and a succession of plagues, of which easily the worst was the Black Death, 1348 – 49, stopped all this in its tracks and some reclaimed land almost certainly reverted to waste.

Even though much of the Heath's true heathland has disappeared, you can still find flora that will tell you where it once was. As you walk uphill from the lower slopes of the Heath

you will notice the occurrence of fine-bladed grasses, mixed patches of clay and sand, indicating the transition from London Clay to Claygate Beds. Once well up on the higher grasslands, you will find sheep's sorrel, those rust red drifts in the summer grass. Damp and boggy patches of lush grass and buttercups indicate a spring line, where rainwater reaches less permeable clay, and further up, bogs and ponds allow wet heathland plants to flourish, such as purple moor grass, bogbean (once used for curing rheumatism) and creeping willow. It is here on the high ground that gorse and heather may still be found, the latter now requiring protection from trampling.

ABOVE AND TOP RIGHT Fine-leaved grasses above the Vale of Health
BOTTOM RIGHT A colony of scabious in the Paddock

ABOVE Sandy Heath, once part of the Common and covered with gorse and heather, is now woodland.
LEFT Gorse, the common shrub of acid soils

The gorse was much more widespread once, with its almost perennial yellow flowers. Gorse burns fast, and was used for kindling and for bread ovens. In lean years the young shoots were pounded and given as fodder to livestock. In the Tudor period London gentry sent their laundry to the washerwomen of Hampstead, who would hang the clean linen out to dry on the gorse bushes in the breeze. Dried in the breeze, the linen would be returned to its owner, fragrant with the sweet honey-coconut scent of the gorse flower.

All that may have disappeared, but one historic memory of the old common heath may be found in the village pound, the brick enclosure just below the Whitestone Pond. Dated 1787, and presumably the last of a succession of village pounds, it was where stray or unauthorized livestock were folded until reclaimed. Illegal grazing was a recurrent problem, not merely in the Middle Ages but even in the nineteenth century. In 1835, for example, the keeper caught a Mr Veale of Fortune Green, who lived up to his name by attempting to pasture fifty cows on the Heath.

Other creatures also inhabit heathland. Some have now gone, such as the adders and possibly also grass snakes, driven out by the sheer quantity of humans. In summer there is still an array of butterflies: the Meadow Brown, the Small Copper, the Speckled Wood and the Orange Tip, as well as crickets, grasshoppers and spiders, all thriving on the unmown grass.

TREES AND WOODLAND

If one looks at an aerial photo of the Heath today, roughly 50 per cent appears wooded. Just over a century ago it would have looked very different, with barely 20 per cent tree cover. At that time the only areas of real woodland were South Wood and North Wood. East Heath, Sandy Heath and West Heath, which made up the common of Hampstead, were virtually treeless. The designed landscapes – Kenwood, Fitzroy Park and Golders Hill had their specimen trees, tree belts and clumps, which marked them out from the former agricultural landscapes. All the rest was fields.

Most of the wooded parts of the Heath today are secondary woodland, where woodland has re-colonized open land, usually land once cleared for farmland or as heathland. As observed earlier, most open land in England will return to woodland if there is no intervention such as mowing or grazing. Here, birch trees have colonized the open sandy ground of West Heath and Sandy Heath, and oak, sycamore and other trees the grassland areas. In some places these areas of secondary woodland hold some gems: for example, old hedgerow lines with rarities such as wild service trees and woodland hawthorns, and ancient oak pollards, trees which were once regularly lopped above browsing height to provide useful wood for staves and implements.

When the Heath became a public open space, the land ceased to be managed as a productive landscape and began to be managed solely for the pleasure of the public. What we have left are the 'ghosts' of previous land use: relict hedgerows, field patterns on Parliament Hill and the Extension, ancient pollards and the bramble- and weed-filled hollows of old sand workings.

In contrast to the secondary woodland, South Wood and North Wood are ancient woods, at least 400 years old and

ABOVE Leaf and flower bud of the wild service tree, an indicator of ancient woodland, though possibly the least known of our native trees
OPPOSITE A lapsed coppiced beech on Sandy Heath

maybe even thousands of years older than that. No individual tree is more than four or five hundred years old, but these woods may have been areas of continuous woodland cover since prehistoric times. It is this lack of disturbance over a long stretch of time which marks them as important habitats. Both woods have been designated Sites of Special Scientific Interest (SSSI), important for their beetles. It is worth pausing a moment to recognize the value of these veteran trees.

Woodland in general in Britain has richer invertebrate fauna than any other habitat. Dead wood, both standing and lying, is vital for fungi as well as invertebrates. For many of these creatures, old trees with stag-headed branches, sap runs, rot holes and cavities are a last refuge in an over-tidy world. In the words of Oliver Rackham, the countryside historian:

> An old tree, especially a pollard, is a world of different habitats each with its special plants and animals: bats roosting in the hollow trunk; hole-nesting birds in smaller cavities; many special beetles and spiders in the red-rotted heartwood of the trunk; peculiar lichens on the ridges and beneath overhangs of old bark. Any old tree should be treasured, for ten thousand young trees do not provide these habitats.

Arguably, more damage was done to woodland habitats in the clearing-up after the great storm in 1987 than was done by the storm itself.

Britain has two native types of oak: the common or pedunculate and the sessile. Both are present here, and both signify something slightly different. The pedunculate oak is more common and is found in wood pastures, in old hedge lines and

ABOVE Wherever possible, fallen trees are now left to provide dead wood habitats for invertebrates.

OPPOSITE Some veteran trees suffer from canopy competition, but dieback is normal in oaks from late middle age.

Pedunculate oak leaves

on boundaries. It colonizes easily in open ground. The sessile, by far the rarer of the two, is found largely in areas of poorer soils and high rainfall and is also the oak of ancient oak and oak–hornbeam woodlands. It does not have the colonizing capacity of the common oak but is more successful at reproduction within woodlands. Sessile oaks are to be found in South Wood. They have never been planted as extensively as the common oak and are largely confined to ancient relict woods as here in South Wood.

'Pedunculate' and 'sessile' indicate the way to tell the two species apart, for pedunculate means 'with a stalk', while sessile means 'without'. The acorn of the pedunculate has a long stalk (peduncle) while the sessile has a very short stalk. To be contrary, the leaf of the pedunculate oak has a short stalk while the leaf of the sessile has a long stalk. Exasperatingly, the two types of oak frequently hybridize.

Up until the second half of the sixteenth century, when the coal economy began to take over, these woods were a productive and vital resource. They were managed to provide fuel, underwood and timber. We know that thousands of fuel faggots were extracted annually from Bishop's Park, just to the north, and the demand, bearing in mind

Sessile oak leaves

ABOVE Chicken-of-the-woods fungus
RIGHT 'Summer darkness', created by overlapping leaves of beech
BELOW The rough bark, nooks and crannies of old trees provide habitats for a huge range of floura and fauna.

BELOW A wood bank in South Wood, probably dating from the late
seventeenth century
OPPOSITE A grove of horse chestnuts on the way to the Ladies' Pond

London's proximity, must have been considerable. Timber would have been extracted for any heavy purpose: the construction of housing, the making of carts and ploughs and so forth. Underwood was also invaluable, cut mainly from coppiced trees that were regularly harvested to provide the basic material for wattle, for fencing or the infilling of timber-frame houses and for almost every conceivable wooden implement. Coppice, of course, had to be fenced in to protect it from grazing livestock. Only when polled trees were above the browse line, as in hedgerows, were they were exposed to grazing.

South Wood was formerly part of a much larger wood, which was in two parts, Cane Wood and Gyll Holt. Cane Wood gave Kenwood its name, and probably derives from *keyne*, the NormanFrench word for oak. Gyll Holt is an Anglo-Saxon place name, indicating a wooded gully. One may hazard a guess, therefore, that it was probably the wooded slopes down to the Highgate Ponds. The likelihood is that ash, alder and willow grew on these wetter slopes. Ash was an extremely useful wood, being springier than oak, and was used extensively for farm implements. Alder proved exceptionally strong, for example for axletrees. A map, dating from *c*.1600, shows the whole wood as divided into ten 18-acre plots. The woodland was thinned or felled on a ten-year rotation, plot by plot.

England is exceptional in northern Europe for its 'veteran' trees, hosting 80 per cent of those growing north of the Pyrenees. Their beauty and their cultural significance have long been appreciated but their scientific importance is only just being understood. The English took an early liking to these ancient trees that looked as if they had been on the landscape for ever. The Heath, not including North Wood or South Wood,

has over 500 veteran trees. Many parts of rural Britain cannot begin to compete with such longevity.

The Heath also contains pockets of exotic and ornamental trees, the evidence of more recent tinkering with the landscape. In both the eighteenth and nineteenth centuries many landed proprietors became avid collectors of exotic species of trees and shrubs, which they planted to enhance their landscape. The Mansfields at Kenwood, the Southamptons at Fitzroy Park and Thomas Spencer Wells at Golders Hill were among them. Exotics were planted for other reasons too. If you walk East Park, above the Viaduct, you will find pseudo-acacias, exotic oaks and maples, descendants of the trees planted by the Lord of the Manor, Sir Thomas Maryon Wilson, in the mid-nineteenth century, in preparation for his villa development (see page 80).

Along the edge of the Upper Fairground stands a row of large oaks. Do not be deceived into thinking that this is an ancient hedgerow line. These are Lucombe oaks, a hybrid between the Turkey oak and the cork oak occurring naturally in southern Europe, but first raised from seed in England in 1765 by Mr Lucombe, an Exeter nurseryman. They, too, were planted by Maryon Wilson, as were various willows, firs and Turkey oaks planted on other parts of the Heath, perhaps to demonstrate his ownership of the Heath.

In the late nineteenth and early twentieth centuries the London County Council planted the small clumps of exotic oaks, pines and copper beeches in the fields of Parliament Hill in the well-intentioned but wholly misguided attempt to 'parkify' the Heath. Despite the outcry from local people who treasured the landscape unblemished by municipal thinking the exotics survived; they are now a kind of historical footnote on the landscape.

Trees, some say, are the lungs of the city, as if every tree by definition is desirable. Trees need well-informed management. Hundreds of sycamore seedlings evoke splutters of outrage from some, but are fiercely defended by others, particularly bird watchers, who know that sycamores host exceptionally large numbers of aphids and are therefore an important food source. Difficult decisions, therefore, need to be made about managing the Heath and felling sufficient new tree growth to ensure the 'architecture' of the Heath – its woodland, heathland and farmland.

OVERLEAF
The LCC tried to 'parkify' the farmland of Parliament Hill by
planting clumps of exotic trees.

THE FARMLANDS

The third 'landscape' of the Heath is that of the farmland which once existed here. The traces and relics of agriculture are still obvious. What is harder to imagine is precisely how the land was used in, say, the Middle Ages. We know that most of the Bagshot Sand was heathland, and that there was plenty of woodland around the sandier upper parts of the Claygate Beds, but to some extent we have to guess about the lower parts, the lower Claygate Beds and the London Clay.

Some things we do indeed know about Hampstead manorial lands. Only half the Heath, as we know it, fell within the Manor of Hampstead. Its boundary ran beside the path running from the Hampstead Gate of South Wood down to Parliament Hill, and down the back of Tanza Road. A manor survey dated 1312 indicates that the Lord of the Manor kept all the land between this boundary and the stream running down from the Vale of Health for his own use; thus it was known as 'demesne' land. The reason is clear: it caught the sun from midday onwards. We also know that he allowed tree growth on the area of the Upper Fairground called Whitebirche Wood; the name indicates the kind of wood that grew most willingly on the transitional Bagshot Sand – Claygate Beds land here. Birch was probably grown for fuel.

Some land may have been used as arable, but one can reasonably reckon the best arable land was on the sunny west- and south-west-facing slopes of the Manor, straddling Fitzjohn's Avenue.

Yet the greater part of the present Heath was probably used even in the Middle Ages as pasture and meadow. By the

The old track through Wyldes Farm, lined by an ancient hedgerow

sixteenth century the City was demanding three vital ingredients from nearby farmland: grazing, dairy products and hay. The grazing was for the herds of livestock the drovers brought down from the north. By the time they reached the villages near London, the livestock badly needed time to fatten up again after the rigours of the journey. So one can imagine Parliament Hill Fields, and the Heath Extension possibly, hosting herds of dairy or transient cattle and sheep, before they were driven on to the Holloway Road and down to Smithfield. With the progressive switch from wood fuel to coal, we know that South Wood was reduced in size in the late seventeenth century, presumably because wood production was becoming less important and could not compete with the value of the land as pasture and hay meadows, producing fodder to be taken into the City.

We know, too, that Lord and Lady Mansfield at Kenwood House played at farming, for example on West Meadow. In this they were following the current fashion of the landed gentry. The Mansfields kept a small herd of Warwickshire Longhorns, chosen not for their milking potential but because they were rated more picturesque 'in a gentleman's park'. By the late 1770s the dairy was the responsibility of a beautiful young woman, Dido Belle, daughter of Lord Mansfield's naval nephew and a black

woman, presumably a slave, captured on a Spanish ship. Dido was brought up from infancy at Kenwood, and greatly doted upon by Lord Mansfield as a member of the family, to the occasional shock of visitors. Indeed, he commissioned a portrait – thought to be by Zoffany – of Dido alongside her cousin Elizabeth, with the Kenwood landscape and St Paul's Cathedral in the background.

Dido had more influence that she can have realized. For when she was only seven, her guardian, now Lord Chief Justice of England, made an historic judgement in ordering the freedom of a runaway slave. Would he have ruled as he did had he not dandled young Dido on his knee and thus learnt the crucial lesson of our common humanity? It is impossible to say, but you will want to know what happened to Dido. She married a John Davinier (perhaps of Huguenot descent) at the ultra-fashionable St George's Hanover Square and begat three strapping sons.

What better harbinger of multicultural Britain could there have been than Dido Belle? But we have strayed far from our farming theme. The Dairy, next to West Meadow, postdates Dido, but serves as a reminder of the dairy-producing landscape that characterized much of the Heath.

We would probably be right in imagining the farmland that now comprises the Heath Extension as also primarily pasture and meadow, although we know there was a Wyldes Wood, where Wildwood Road now runs. This all fell inside Wyldes Farm, lying just inside the Manor of Hendon. From the mid-fifteenth century until purchased by the LCC in 1907, Wyldes belonged to Eton College. We know about Wyldes Wood principally because a tenant, John Slannyng, got into hot water for felling 34 acres of it; the story is indicative of the wood's once substantial size. Turner's Wood, hidden behind the houses on the east side of Wildwood Road, is probably a remnant of this wood.

LEFT An ancient boundary oak, marking the manorial boundary
RIGHT Wyldes Farm, probably dating from the early seventeenth century

Wonderfully, the seventeenth-century Wyldes farmhouse still survives, now known as Old Wyldes, standing at the junction of Hampstead Way and Wildwood Road. Next door stands Wyldes, its barn. They survive by a whisker of good fortune (see page 88).

What we have left of the farmland on the lower slopes of both the north and south sides of the Hampstead–Highgate ridge are the surviving hedgerows, many of them in highly visible form. Most of these are simply field enclosures, compartmentalizing the landscape. Some are now camouflaged in secondary woodland and demand a more careful eye. Suddenly one can notice a line of mature oaks running straight among other tree growth. Often they grow out of a slight undulation,

the last gasp of the hedgerow bank and ditch. Centuries ago the ditch would have been scoured and the hedge carefully maintained to ensure a proper enclosure and to deter livestock from breaking through the thicket.

The oldest trees of the Heath are not woodland but these hedgerow and boundary trees. Most are oak pollards, which probably grew up protected from grazing livestock within hedgerows. Once an oak had grown above the browse line, the branches would be cropped every ten or so years. Without any records of their planting we can only guess at the age of these oaks, probably between 300 and 500 years old. Some of these ancient hedgerow trees are surprisingly small and stunted and difficult to identify in the middle of recent secondary woodland.

An old hedgerow line of wild service trees and oaks

How were these hedges made? We know that hedgerows were sometimes deliberately planted to keep animals in, while others on arable lands grew up surreptitiously along the edges of open fields where no one had ploughed. Yet there is evidence to suppose that some field boundaries on Hampstead Heath were largely the result of 'assarts', open fields created by the deliberate cutting down of woodland while a line of trees was left to form the hedge boundary. The vital clue for this supposition lies in the presence of two species of tree. These are the wild service tree and the woodland, or midland, hawthorn, both woodland trees and thus indicators of a former wooded landscape.

Even before 1066, the landscape had been divided into estates, later called 'manors' by the Normans and each an economic enterprise. The system was the basis of society as well as the economy. Most estates contained the three elements we see on Hampstead Heath: heath or waste, woodland and agricultural lands. The Lord of the Manor would allow his tenants to use the common waste, and to grow crops on the common field. He reserved for his own use the best agricultural land and also the woodland, although tenants might be given rights to garner fallen dead wood.

A major concern was to ensure that the whole estate's boundaries were properly defined, since an ambitious manorial neighbour might well encroach. In the case of Hampstead we are fortunate, for we have a description dated AD 986, which refers to the manorial boundaries, traces of which can still be found without too much difficulty. The most obvious section is the eastern boundary running south across the Heath, still marked by a ditch dating back to Saxon times. This ditch separated the manor from Highgate, known then as Tottenhall Manor. Beside the ditch are old oak trees which themselves became boundary markers. Oak trees were often used to mark parish boundaries. When the bounds were 'beaten' annually in the spring, prayers and gospel readings for a good harvest would often be said while standing by a boundary oak; hence 'Gospel Oak'. This boundary runs around the north side of Kenwood's West Meadow, along the watershed down to the edge of South Hill Park and then down the back of Tanza Road on Parliament Hill. In the eighteenth and nineteenth centuries the boundary oaks were augmented by stone markers, and at the beginning of the twentieth century by metal posts. This boundary remained the substantive border for a thousand years, at the end between the boroughs of Hampstead and St Pancras, until both were absorbed into the Borough of Camden in 1965.

Boundaries: ditches and oak trees gave way to more formal markers, stones installed by each parish and, later, metal posts by the LCC.

THE HOUSES AND LANDSCAPES OF THE NORTHERN HEIGHTS

In the seventeenth century very few people actually lived along the Hampstead–Highgate ridge. It was felt remote, partly because the heathland was favoured by footpads as good territory for the ambush of travellers. There were only one or two houses, of which the most notable was at Kenwood, built by James I's printer, John Bill, after he acquired the estate in 1616.

During the eighteenth century, however, there was a growing interest in the scenic landscape, in stark contrast with the passion for enclosed and geometrically planned gardens of previous centuries. The idea of making gardens blend into an idealized landscape beyond revolutionized garden design. As Horace Walpole said of William Kent, an early exponent of the new fashion, he 'leaped the fence and saw that all nature was a garden'.

So it was inevitable that the Hampstead–Highgate ridge, the Northern Heights, should become a favoured vantage point, with its stunning views down to the City or northwards into countryside. By the last years of the century the prime sites overlooking London had been filled, from west to east, by Thomas Erskine, the Lord Chancellor, at Evergreen Hill (beside the Spaniards Inn), the Earl of Mansfield at Kenwood and Lord Southampton at Fitzroy Park (on the slopes of Highgate). All three sought the assistance of the landscape designer Humphry Repton. Only his advice to Mansfield has survived, in one of his 'Red Books', his famous trademark dossier, so named on account of their red morocco binding, containing his advice and plans for

Hampstead Lane originally ran close to the north front of Kenwood House. It was moved to its present route between 1793 and 1796.

his clients. Mansfield's Red Book and other pieces of evidence indicate how Repton ensured a symbiotic visual relationship, with these three estates facing the City and merging seamlessly.

Erskine's garden was modest, and only accessible through a tunnel under the Spaniards Road. Yet even he could look out on Mansfield's pastures grazed by the Warwickshire Longhorns, acquired for their Arcadian loveliness. Erskine's eye would then be drawn into the distance, to Southampton's villa of Fitzroy House on the slopes of Highgate Hill.

At Mansfield's Kenwood Repton saw his task as transforming what had 'hitherto been considered a mere villa' into a country residence that suggested elegance and importance. He replaced the enclosed garden with a sweeping lawn and even suggested screening Kentish Town 'to create the illusion that Kenwood extended almost to the City of London'. To left and to right, Mansfield's view let on to the respective Southampton and Erskine estates.

The eye is deliberately enticed to explore the landscape.

ABOVE The tumulus remains a perennial tease.
OPPOSITE A mystery of Sandy Heath, the avenue behind Heath House. Who planted it, and why?

Southampton's landscape at Fitzroy Park is the hardest to imagine because one can no longer stand close to the site of the house. The approach is still called Fitzroy Park, at the end of Millfield Lane. Described as a beautiful rustic villa, it looked south-west, enjoying long views through parkland trees and across the Highgate Ponds to Parliament Hill Fields and the tumulus. The tumulus itself was probably constructed in the early eighteenth century as a focal point, perhaps with a suggestion of 'ancient Britain'. Southampton had only a few years to enjoy his villa and his park, for he died in 1797, and the house was demolished in the late 1820s and the estate broken up.

Golders Hill, one of two large estates facing northwards, is a landscape that has lost its house. Built in the 1760s, it was later owned by John Coore, who also sought landscape advice from Humphry Repton. The house was greatly enlarged in the mid-nineteenth century by Sir Thomas Spencer Wells, Surgeon to the Queen's Household. The ancient oaks in Golders Hill Park date from before the creation of the park. Indeed, if you explore its southern boundary, you may still find veteran oaks growing on the bank and ditch that formed the old manorial boundary between Hampstead and Hendon, a boundary that predates the Norman Conquest. In 1941 the house, standing on the high ground just inside the main entrance, was destroyed by a parachute mine.

ABOVE Golders Hill Park
OPPOSITE The lime avenue, the old route to North End before North End Way was cut through the hillside

The house on the other estate, the Hill, was also built in the eighteenth century, but rebuilt in the 1890s and in 1905 acquired by the soap magnate Lord Leverhulme. Leverhulme loved throwing lavish parties in his garden, which enjoyed spectacular views northwards. Yet he was anxious to ensure privacy for his guests from gawping hoi polloi out for a stroll on West Heath. So he commissioned Thomas Mawson, a man with a reputation as 'the landscape architect of the Empire', to solve the problem.

Over the next twenty years Mawson laid out the gardens and created a remarkable 800 feet long Italianate pergola on a raised terrace, using the timely spoil from the tunnel being dug to run the Northern Line as far as Golders Green. The pergola section of the garden became accessible to the public in 1963. Over the years the pergola fell into disrepair: columns collapsed and the retaining wall began to slip and crumble. Restoration was undertaken by the Corporation of London and in 1995 the pergola re-opened to the public. Cleverly, the pergola's orientation affords us a view over West Heath but privacy from our prying eyes for the residents of the house, renamed Inverforth House, and which, although now broken up into flats, retains its air of exclusivity.

HOW THE HEATH WAS SAVED

We owe our enjoyment of the Heath to the passion aroused for its survival in the nineteenth century. All around London, lords of manors were cashing in on the rocketing demand for land for housing, selling off both their own demesne land and the common land on which tenants had customarily grazed their animals. Sir Thomas Maryon Wilson, Hampstead's absentee lord, was no different.

Maryon Wilson, however, had been restricted by his father's will, to sell any part of the estate and restricted leases to twenty-one years' duration. He faced a yet more formidable problem in a growing constituency of articulate and well-connected professional people who treasured the common heathland. When, in 1829, he tried to clear the way ahead to develop the common heath with a private bill before Parliament, the best connected of Hampstead residents managed to get the bill thrown out. Perhaps his most formidable opponent was the 3rd Earl of Mansfield at Kenwood House, who repeatedly thwarted him, in 1830, 1843 and 1844. Furthermore, on each occasion local opposition grew stronger. The principal objection was to his intention to develop the common land.

In his frustration, Maryon Wilson decided to exploit the sand of Sandy Heath, which was now excavated on an unprecedented scale. He also started to change the character of the Heath by planting exotic trees, for example the pines overlooking the Vale of Health, the line of Lucombe oaks on the Fairground and one or two false acacias. This was his own demesne land, the land described on page 61, where Whitebirche Wood once stood. Maryon Wilson planned an exclusive estate of twenty-eight villas, each with two acres of garden, and called it East Park. He commenced by laying a drive all the way down to the Hampstead Ponds, now the principal north–south cycle track on the Heath. He built the Viaduct to carry this drive across the swampy ground, which he turned into an ornamental pond. Maryon Wilson began construction of the Viaduct flamboyantly in early September 1845. *The Times* sent a correspondent along to see the fun:

> . . . yesterday was fixed for the laying of the first stone . . . a considerable number of persons had assembled to witness the ceremony. The hour fixed was 2 o'clock for 3; and shortly before the latter hour a band of musicians marched to the ground and began to amuse the assembled company by a variety of lively airs, not forgetting the never tiring polka. They were followed by a party of amateur artillery, who mounted their pieces on the heights, ready to announce the auspicious event by a discharge of cannon. In a few minutes Sir Thomas Maryon Wilson and a numerous party of relatives and friends arrived; among them was his sister, Mrs Drummond, a charming lady who had been selected to lay the first stone . . . She spread the mortar with a silver trowel made for the occasion, in a most business-like manner, and the level having been applied, struck the stone three times, with a precision that called forth a hearty burst of cheers, and the block was let down to its resting place amid a discharge of cannon and continued cheering, the band meanwhile playing the national anthem.

The keeper's lodge for the proposed villa development of East Park

Fortunately, it required a good deal more than pyrotechnics to complete the project. The ground proved so marshy that the excavations repeatedly collapsed and shortly after the three years it took to complete construction of the Viaduct, Maryon Wilson ran out of money. In the meantime defence of the Heath had become a *cause célèbre*.

Thwarted at every turn, Maryon Wilson laid into the Heath in earnest. That was when he sold off the Bagshot Sands of Sandy Heath to the Midland Railway Company for its construction of the line into St Pancras Station. The removal of thirty cartloads of sand daily from Sandy Heath left the landscape fundamentally changed, the ground now falling away steeply from the Spaniards Road and pockmarked with lunar craters. He also exploited the Claygate Beds, because they made ideal brick earth, giving a twenty-one year lease to a local builder. A great swathe of land below the Viaduct Pond was devoted to brick making. You will still come across half-buried bits of spoilt brick, particularly on the Boundary Path, which crosses the old brickfield. You may have noticed how the Sports Field is cut sharply into the escarpment. It is an attempt to make a virtue out of the excavation of brick earth here.

The Viaduct and pond

Fortunately for the Heath, Maryon Wilson died in 1869 and his brother was happy to sell the common land to the Metropolitan Board of Works. The Hampstead Heath Bill of 1871 stipulated that:

the Board shall at all times preserve, as far as may be, the natural aspect and state of the Heath, and to that end shall protect the turf, heather, timber and other trees, shrubs and brushwood thereon.

The fate of the East Park brickfield, however, still hung in the balance.

At the same time there were growing fears regarding the intentions of the 4th Earl of Mansfield, who owned all the land of the Heath on the east side of the path running south from Hampstead Gate to the bottom of Parliament Hill. The fear was that he might sell everything out of sight of Kenwood House, namely the lands south of South Wood, including Parliament Hill.

Hampstead Heath's saviours, of whom Octavia Hill is the most famous, realized that to secure one side of the boundary between Maryon Wilson's and Mansfield's estates without securing the other would hugely increase the latter's developmental value. All the way down the west side of East Park lay the Heath as protected by the 1871 Act, and at the bottom, beyond the Hampstead Ponds, the manorial land had passed into the hands of a man who built South Hill Park that same year, 1871. Thus the only southern access to East Park, now necessarily avoiding the common heath, would have to be through Mansfield's estate down the east side of East Park. The road up Parliament Hill from South End clearly anticipated Mansfield's predicted development of Parliament Hill Fields – precisely what the Heath conservationists feared.

Lord Mansfield, however, was not predictable. On the contrary, he decided to protect the southern approaches to Kenwood by selling Parliament Hill Fields to the conservationists. This decision was a fatal blow to plans for the belated development of East Park. Not only had a southern approach to East Park ceased to be an option, but the means whereby drainage could feed into London's new sewage system was also obstructed by South Hill Park. East Park, far from being a highly desirable piece of real estate, had suddenly become almost worthless.

Mansfield and the Maryon Wilson estate sold the adjoining lands of Parliament Hill Fields and East Park in 1889 for money raised by local government and individual gifts. Thus by the end of the century Hampstead Heath was an open expanse of 481 acres, albeit still without the grounds of Kenwood House and the land east and south-east of it.

The struggle to rescue open country from development now switched northwards. First, Golders Hill fell into jeopardy following Sir Thomas Spencer Wells' death in 1897. The house and park were put up for auction at a time when developers were competing fiercely for such prime sites for housing. Golders Hill was saved, thanks to the timely intervention of a soap magnate, Thomas Barratt. Barratt was not only the Chairman of A. & F. Pears but also Hampstead's leading historian.

RIGHT Sandy Heath, part of the manorial common, was sold to the Metropolitan Board of Works in 1871.
OVERLEAF Parliament Hill, added to the Heath in 1889

St Jude's, designed by Edwin Lutyens as the centrepiece of the Garden Suburb, planned as an urban arcadia

OPPOSITE
A gazebo on Unwin's Great Wall, inspired by medieval Bavarian hilltop towns

When the bidding at auction outstripped the funds collected by local residents, Barratt stepped in and bid on his own account. In 1899 the house and park were handed to the LCC for use as a public park. When the house was destroyed by a parachute mine in 1941, the park lost its focal point.

In 1902 the Charing Cross, Euston & Hampstead Railway Company obtained consent by Act of Parliament to extend the line north of Hampstead and to build stations at North End and Golders Green. Furthermore, it proposed to destroy Wyldes Farm in the process. Negotiations were already under way between the railway company and Eton College, the owner of the Wyldes estate. But the company had not bargained for the formidable powers of Henrietta Barnett, whose view from her house near the Spaniards Inn would change from Arcadian fields to the red roofs of suburbia. Mrs Barnett moved fast and skilfully. Having created the Hampstead Heath Extension Council, composed principally of local people, she proposed to Eton the purchase of the 80 acres of Wyldes farmland adjacent to Sandy Heath. Her skill lay in proposing simultaneously a model 'garden suburb for all classes', which immediately won her the support of the two borough councils of Hendon and Hampstead, as well as of the LCC.

Athlone House

It was with the prospect of this attractive double scheme that Eton College fell captive to Mrs Barnett's blandishments. The money was raised just before the agreed deadline, and the estate handed over to the LCC in 1907. The land that was obtained was wider than the Extension as we have it, but part of the deal was to construct houses facing on to the Extension on either side and, beyond it to the north, an idealized garden suburb. Barnett took a strong interest in the quality of the housing. Raymond Unwin, an unusually able and socially committed architect, was commissioned to design the suburb, and it was he who designed the 'Great Wall', a high brick wall romantically studded with pavilions and gazebos. Sadly, only a third of the wall was completed before the war in 1914 killed the rest of the project. Unwin was also thwarted in the vistas he wanted from the closes that led down to the Great Wall, However, he did manage to achieve the vista of the central gateway with its elegant shallow steps leading the eye up to the

Lutyens-designed church of St Jude. As for the Extension itself, it has become a poor relation to the rest of the Heath, even though it can boast the best surviving and most obvious ancient hedgerow lines, the closest we get on the Heath to farmed countryside.

Finally, the Kenwood estate fell into jeopardy. The 6th Earl of Mansfield had no interest in Kenwood, much preferring life at his Perthshire seat, Scone Palace. For a while he let the Kenwood estate. The Grand Duke Michael Alexandrovich, younger brother of the Czar Nicholas, for example, took the house and grounds during the years 1909 to 1917. Grand Duke Michael was a disgraced exile, having committed the grave solecism of a relationship with a twice-divorced commoner, by whom he had a son and whom he eventually married. He was a sporty type, perhaps the only Russian addicted to that most English of games, cricket. He also enjoyed a round of golf, which he did very ably on South Meadow. He was sufficiently tall that

Witanhurst House, with St Michael's Church behind

he could swing only bespoke lengthened clubs. In 1917, however, the house fell formally vacant, for Michael had returned to Russia to fight on the outbreak of war in 1914, a fact which calls for a minor diversion. It was Michael's misfortune that in March 1917, under pressure from the Duma, Czar Nicholas abdicated in his favour. Since this was automatically opposed by Kerensky, Michael immediately renounced the throne. Inevitably, however, he remained a marked man. Following the Bolshevik Revolution, his end was only a matter of time. In June 1918, Michael was abducted, shot and his body burnt, almost certainly by the secret police.

Back to Kenwood where, whether he had learnt of the Grand Duke Michael's fate or not, Mansfield now decided to seek a purchaser for the estate. Since this included South Meadow to the south of South Wood, the character of much of the Heath, most notably the rest of Parliament Hill Fields and the upper end of East Park, was gravely imperilled.

It was another soap magnate, Arthur Crosfield, who came to the rescue. Crosfield lived at Witanhurst, on Highgate's West Hill. He knew the ground very well, since his passion for golf had led inevitably to a good friendship with the Grand Duke Michael on South Meadow. With a sale seemingly imminent, he quickly co-opted his neighbours Robert Waley-Cohen (Caen Wood Towers, now Athlone House) and Henry Goodison (Fitzroy Park) to establish the Kenwood Preservation Council. On this occasion no local government funds were forthcoming. Unable to raise sufficient money, in 1922 the Kenwood Preservation Council negotiated the purchase of two fields, South Meadow and part of Lord Southampton's former parkland, now known as Cohen's Fields. One might have thought these two plots were the least interesting acquisitions, but Crosfield knew what he was doing. The acquisition of these two parcels of land left the rest of Kenwood with major drainage problems. The Preservation Council then struck a deal with Mansfield. In return

for Mansfield's covenant for the permanent conservation of a strip of South Wood to protect the view northwards from South Meadow, it now undertook to support Mansfield in his bid to persuade the LCC to allow him to lay a drain across the Heath to the Vale of Health sewer. In all probability the Preservation Council already knew that the LCC was not persuadable; indeed it is likely it quietly ensured it was not persuadable before agreeing to this deal. Realizing the game was up, Mansfield agreed to sell all of South Wood and also the Pasture Ground in 1924. In the meantime the Earl of Iveagh negotiated the purchase of Kenwood House to accommodate his collection of pictures, which he intended to bequeath to the nation, so this last part of the estate became public property soon after his death in 1927.

Yet we might have inherited more. In 1854 a city barrister, who declined to disclose his identity, wrote to *The Times*:

> The public should purchase, while it can be had on comparatively moderate terms, all the open ground between Primrose Hill and Hampstead Heath. This land belongs, starting from the hill, the first portion to the Provost and Fellows of Eton College; the second portion to the Dean and Chapter of Westminster; and the third, the fields in question, to Sir Thomas Wilson . . . The Regent's Park would thus be continued to Hampstead-heath. Another such glorious opportunity of forming the finest park . . . in the world may never occur again.

Indeed, alas, it did not. Yet how we have what we have remains an astonishing tale of foresight, dogged planning, philanthropy and energy. We have much for which to be grateful.

THE PEOPLE'S PLEASURE GROUND

Many people think of the Heath as a relic of the pre-urban landscape. However, remarkable as the Heath landscape undoubtedly is, it is also an oasis, packed with a great quantity of people and filled with an astonishing variety of human activity.

Long before the Heath was saved, Londoners were already beginning to use it to escape the grime of the city. Donkey rides were a feature on the Heath by the 1820s, their numbers increasing to such an extent that Dickens commented, 'the donkey is truly the indigenous animal of Hampstead Heath'. It was only after the Heath came into public ownership that the activities of the donkey owners could be controlled. Two stands were established, for 45 donkeys near the Vale of Health and another 60 at the bottom of Downshire Hill.

From 1860 when it was laid, the North London Line provided the principal access to the Heath. By the 1880s a fine bank holiday might draw up to 100,000 people to the Heath, 'the Place to Ruralize'. And by this time, too, the small fairs held at South End Green in the middle years of the century had metamorphosed into huge and wonderfully vulgar events held on the Heath, one on the heights overlooking the Vale of Health pond, and the other at the foot of Downshire Hill. The fair continues to this day, vulgarity written into the Heath tradition.

Today, the Heath hosts as many as 10 million visits each year. Most people come simply to stroll, to jog or to walk their dog. Others come for more energetic activities, mainly innocent ones like jogging or swimming, but a few come on to the Heath for darker pursuits. Suicide, murder and infanticide have all happened on the Heath. With luck the violence proves harmless.

Parliament Hill

Early on a cold December morning in 1839 two men with more testosterone than common sense met on the Heath to settle 'an alleged debt of honour'. It was Christmas Eve and perhaps the thought of the Christ child weakened their sense of purpose, for 'Both fired without taking effect.' Their seconds negotiated an amicable arrangement and they doubtless repaired to a local hostelry for a hearty breakfast and became firm friends ever after.

As for little boys on the Heath, in the words of one indignant correspondent to *The Times* in 1911, 'The boy is at heart a barbarian, and it is only by a process of evolution that he becomes civilised.' Until that civilizing mission was accomplished 'the West Heath should be absolutely forbidden to children under 16 years of age'. Some might now think that the West Heath should be banned to boys *over* sixteen years of age.

Which takes one from violence to the question of sex, another hotly pursued activity on the Heath. Lustful limbs have always throbbed in the summer undergrowth, either by *force majeure* or by mutual consent. In May 1919 at Hampstead Police Court at the top of Downshire Hill, 'the acting Chairman said the Bench were determined to stamp out immorality in Hampstead. Three men and three women were charged with improper behaviour on Hampstead Heath.' Ten years later, in 1927, the Women's Freedom League were lobbying the police because parents were afraid to let their children play on the Heath because of the number of offences against children. It seems to have been a peak year for bad behaviour on the Heath. Following the Easter weekend no fewer than eighty-six people were up before the beak, mainly it seems for the use of 'water-squirts' by that particularly miscreant category of humanity, youths. Their defence to the Bench was ingenious: 'that if the squirts could not be used, their sale should be prohibited'. When it comes to human behaviour, there is not much new that happens on the Heath.

One of the remarkable characteristics of the Heath is that almost anything done on it will cause a splutter of outrage in some quarter. One hundred and twenty-five years ago it was still commonplace everywhere in England for men to swim naked, not least in the upper Hampstead (now Mixed Bathing) Pond, which had been used for swimming since the 1820s, if not earlier. But with public ownership of the Heath, the prudes soon went on the offensive, in July 1872 one of them being moved to write to *The Times*:

> Sir, – At six o'clock last Sunday afternoon, taking a walk on this Heath, which has been entrusted to the Metropolitan Board of Works to maintain good order for the 'unrestricted exercise and recreation of the public' I have been more shocked and disgusted than I can find words to express. Imagine, if you can, a . . . few ladies and gentlemen, numbers of children, and a hundred or so of the 'public' strolling near the pond, and some 50 perfectly naked men and boys bathing in the pond and running about the banks among the bystanders in a state of absolute nudity.

The prudes prevailed to the extent that swimmers covered their nakedness, but they failed to stop the swimming itself, which they probably also found indecent. The Hampstead Mixed Bathing Pond continued as a regular venue for outdoor swimmers. In 1893 the Highgate (now Men's) Bathing Pond was opened, and it was here that then-famous Swedish divers demonstrated to an astonished London public what serious stuff could be achieved from a great height, inspiring the formation of the Amateur Diving Association. In 1923 a concrete Olympic-standard diving board was constructed and the Highgate Diving Club established, the first of its kind in Britain. By this time races on Christmas morning had been attracting the hardy for a good twenty years. The Ladies' Bathing Pond opened in the early 1920s, one early swimmer recalling the 'small fry which used to terrify the women when they swam down their cleavages'. But it was the pike that proved a more serious threat. One young swimmer who disregarded the lifeguard's warning not to tempt pike by dangling her toes in the water suddenly leapt in the air and hopped around on one foot screaming. She was taken off to hospital, badly bitten. Pike are now periodically fished out, to

lurk in toe-less waters elsewhere. Among the more famous who risked all in the Ladies' Pond was the actress Katharine Hepburn, who made a point of swimming there, even in her seventies, when staying in London.

In 1937 an open air 'lido' was opened at the foot of Parliament Hill to provide a much more extensive swimming facility, appealing to those who deprecate the murk of nature or the snapping jaws of pike.

Periodically, the Mixed Bathing Pond has given rise to exasperation. In 1932 Professor Joad wrote to the *Ham and High*:

> So extreme is the terror of the LCC of an overlap between the sexes that no man may enter the Hampstead enclosure for a bathe after 8am, though no woman may approach it before 9am . . . The proximity of men and women in process of uncovering their bodies, which unfortunately is a necessary preliminary of immersion, is felt to create so alarming a situation . . . that it must at all costs be prevented.

He had a point, since men and women were already well screened by a partition. But possibly the LCC had a point also. More recently the lifeguards at the Ladies' Pond have taken what they call 'fanny walks' on the Meadow and Small Meadow to ensure no nude sunbathing. Meanwhile, the Men's Bathing Pond has become a favoured gay scene where those with well-toned torsos strut their stuff and since 1994 one section of the Pond enclosure has been dedicated to nude sunbathing, becoming the only public nudist facility in London. Beyond the confines of these ponds, the social mores allow a greater degree of nakedness than ever before. The custodians of morality half a century ago would have had a fit, but probably not Professor

Joad, who considered nudism an aphrodisiac but also a distraction to the intellect.

The Heath has also witnessed more stirring sights. Following the formation of the West Middlesex Rifle Volunteers in 1859, Major Compton took his chaps out on to the Heath to display their prowess:

> An enemy was posted . . . on a hill, on the one hand, and on the other, an attacking force occupied a position in the vale whose object it was to dislodge him, and with that view threw out skirmishers, who were attended by regular covering parties, and supported by a reserve. For upwards of an hour a brisk fusillade was kept up, with blank cartridge of course, and some volley firing, given with admirable precision, the enemy at length beating a retreat.

In the First World War troops again used the Heath for training, to the wry amusement of *The Times* correspondent:

> There were great hidings, and trackings, and ambushes in days long before the Boy Scouts came to play the old delightful games with a new seriousness . . . [And now] you may hear an officer gravely say, 'The enemy are supposed to be behind that hill' and the mind flies back to days when the enemy, in knickerbockers or in skimpy skirts, was indeed behind the same hill, and the intrepid attacking force took its orders from a four-foot captain no whit less earnest than this one of the moustache and straps. The children stop their playing to look at these grown and bronzed men playing so splendidly on these best of playgrounds the best of games.

And doubtless today's 'barbarian' boys still play such games.

ABOVE AND LEFT Parliament Hill
RIGHT Near the Men's Pond

The Heath Extension

Soldiers manoeuvred on the Heath, but socialist politicians began their own campaign, creating a kind of speaker's corner on the south-eastern slopes of Parliament Hill Fields (still marked by a small whitewashed obelisk) where they could rally the comrades with fiery messages of class solidarity.

In March 1950 a remarkable sporting event took place on the Heath, requiring plenty of skill and testosterone: the London ski-jumping competition. For Londoners it was more showcase than competition, for every competitor was Norwegian and the very first to jump was a mere thirteen years old. A more recent winter sports innovation has been the installation of an ice rink at the foot of Parliament Hill Fields during the Christmas–New Year season. Such things may largely pass people by. Yet kites continue to be flown, joggers continue to run, hopeful anglers still try to catch the last tiddler, bigger children still climb trees and smaller ones continue to feed the ducks.

A hardy perennial, ever since the Heath became a public domain, is the quarrel about how to use and maintain it. Indignant expostulations in the press started almost immediately. In 1871 one correspondent complained to *The Times* that almost six months after the Heath had become public:

No constables have been appointed . . . Gypsies and idlers still cook their meals at the expense of the fences on the

Sandy Heath

adjacent fields and gardens. Bird trapping and shooting are unchecked. Trees and shrubs are damaged without hindrance or restraint

On the other hand, when the Board of Works finally rolled into action to plant specified (and demanded) ornamental grounds, others saw red. Cutting or lopping trees unleashed howls of outrage:

There was a time when they [the trees] were regarded as beautiful parts of a beautiful scene – admired by Turner, Constable and Callcott, each and all of whom delighted to perpetuate them on canvas. Now they all appear but little better than the trees of a German box of toys fixed upon stands to secure an upright position.

The fight has lost little of its vigour since then. In 1978 *The Times* reported a widespread indignation with the GLC's management of the Heath. One local naturalist pronounced that 'The whole area has become an arboreal slum, with overcrowding of trees we don't want such as sycamores.' He had a point: the unmanaged growth of trees had indeed eroded the once sharply different landscapes – heath, farmland and woodland. In the meantime, the bird lobby was furious about

OPPOSITE The Fair
BELOW The Boating Pond

other trees being lopped. Robert Dougall, former President of the RSPB, for example, complained at the removal of willows around one particular pond with a real conversation stopper: 'I saw one of the grebes there last month, and the look on its face was unbelievable.'

Birds immediately evoke the name of Kate Springett. It was by force of personality that Springett, by profession a milliner, by hobby an ornithologist, became the official GLC bird observer on the Heath. In her passion for birds, some felt she was blind to other facets of the Heath:

> 'We've got what we call our "Katie areas" for Miss Springett,' exclaimed one exasperated manager, 'but the whole thing is a compromise. If you want to let Hampstead Heath become a jungle, then fine for the bird watchers – but what about the runners? I tell you, I'm inundated with so many letters from people I can't get on with my job . . . and I'm tired of people criticising me for getting rid of nettles that might provide food for the lesser chiff-chaff.'

Kate Springett was herself capable of reducing things to farce and Monty Python's dead parrot sketch springs to mind:

> So highly is she regarded that, at her request, the GLC sent round a squad to remove a dead owl from her tree. 'Madam,' they said, 'it is not dead, it is merely asleep.' 'Nonsense, poke it,' she replied. They did, and the owl flew off in a disgruntled manner.

And doubtless, the look on its face, too, was unbelievable.

Since then the City of London has assumed the management and it now takes the flak, as may be seen from time to time in the columns of the *Ham and High*. Of one thing the Corporation may indeed be sure: as long as there is a Heath, there will be Heath-lovers, who will argue with great passion about how it should be managed. Some will generate wisdom concerning it, others plenty of hot air. And without its population of devotees with their astonishing range of activity, it would scarcely be the Heath.

RIGHT Ladies' Pond Meadow
BELOW Parliament Hill

INDEX